To:_____

From:_____

mom's
going
WiLD

(again)

SOURCEBOOKS, INC.®
NAPERVILLE, ILLINOIS

Copyright © 2004 by Sourcebooks, Inc.
Cover and internal design © 2004 by Sourcebooks, Inc.
Cover photo © 2004 by Workbook Stock
Internal photos © 2004 by CSA Images
Sourcebooks and the colophon are registered trademarks of
Sourcebooks, Inc.

Published by Sourcebooks, Inc.
P.O. Box 4410, Naperville, Illinois 60567-4410
(630) 961-3900
FAX: (630) 961-2168
www.sourcebooks.com

Library of Congress Cataloging-in-Publication Data

Mom's going wild again / by Sourcebooks, Inc.
    p. cm.
  ISBN 1-40220-088-9 (alk. paper)
  1. Mothers—Humor. 2. Motherhood—Humor. I. Sourcebooks, Inc.
PN6231.M68 M64 2004
818'.602—dc2'

                              2003020089

        Printed and bound in the United States of America
            LB   10   9   8   7   6   5   4   3   2   1

"Motherhood is the second oldest profession in the world."

—Erma Bombeck

"Never lend your car to anyone to whom you have given birth."

-Erma Bombeck

What a cool car.
It's been years since you rode in
a convertible with the top down, or up,
for that matter. Are those boys talking to you?
Couldn't be—the car is slowing down. Your mind
goes into a time warp, especially when you hear
Beach Boys blaring from the car radio, until you
realize the car's driven by the boy who baby-sits
your kids. Go for a ride? Oh, yeah, off you
go, whipping your hair into one of your
daughter's scrunchies and adjusting
your sunglasses for
maximum cool.

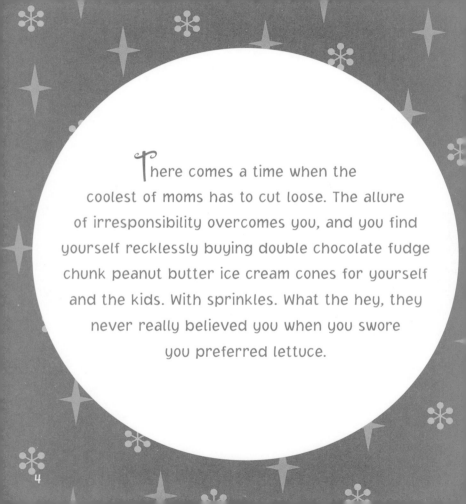

There comes a time when the coolest of moms has to cut loose. The allure of irresponsibility overcomes you, and you find yourself recklessly buying double chocolate fudge chunk peanut butter ice cream cones for yourself and the kids. With sprinkles. What the hey, they never really believed you when you swore you preferred lettuce.

"A mother is never cocky or proud, because she knows the school principal may call at any minute to report that her child has just driven a motorcycle through the gymnasium."

–Mary Kay Blakely

"The most important thing she'd learned over the years was that there was no way to be a perfect mother and a million ways to be a good one."

—Jill Churchill

You're in the local House of Electronics, shopping for a teeny, tiny, one-of-a-kind plastic part, only available at your local House of Electronics (unless you actually live in Japan), without which your entire home entertainment system is a useless pile of landfill. As far as your jaded eye can see, television screens are filled with teenagers on a beach in scanty bathing suits, jumping up and down, doing something with shaving cream for prize money.

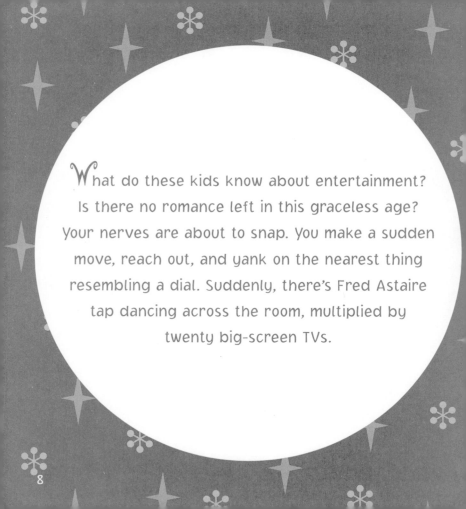

What do these kids know about entertainment? Is there no romance left in this graceless age? Your nerves are about to snap. You make a sudden move, reach out, and yank on the nearest thing resembling a dial. Suddenly, there's Fred Astaire tap dancing across the room, multiplied by twenty big-screen TVs.

"Reminds me of what one of mine wrote in a third-grade piece on how her mother spent her time. She reported 'one half time on home, one half time on outside things, one half time writing.'"

—Charlotte Montgomery

"Mothers had a thousand thoughts to get through with in a day, and...most of these were about avoiding disaster."

-Natalie Kusz

It's a miracle; but there they are—
Fred and Ginger—and your childhood tap
classes come flooding back to you. There's only
one thing to do. Your kids stare in amazement as
your softshoe routine starts to draw a small but
admiring crowd. Your kids didn't know you could
tap dance—of course, the subject never came
up. You hope you're not creating a moment
that will scar them for life.

They still haven't quite recovered from the time you dressed as Pat Benatar in a leopard-skin unitard and went on stage at the Lion's Club talent night singing "Heartbreaker." Flamboyant? Maybe. You figure the best reason to wear a leopard-skin unitard is because...you can.

"A woman came to ask the doctor if a woman should have children after thirty-five. I said thirty-five is enough for any woman!"

–Gracie Allen

"What do you get
on Mother's Day?
A card with flowers
that are made out of pink
toilet paper—
a lot of pink toilet paper.
You get breakfast in bed.
Then you get up and fix
everybody else their breakfast.
And then you go to the bathroom
and you're out of toilet paper."

—Liz Scott

$\mathcal{Y}$es, you remember another time you danced with abandon—it was a summer evening at an outdoor theater. At intermission, the lines for the Porto-Potties were long, but the night was balmy and music wafted over you and your husband as he earnestly explained the plot to you. There was nothing to do but dance, and you and he cut a fine figure as you swirled and dipped until the boy's and girl's lines diverged. Anybody who got stepped on seemed to accept it in good spirits.

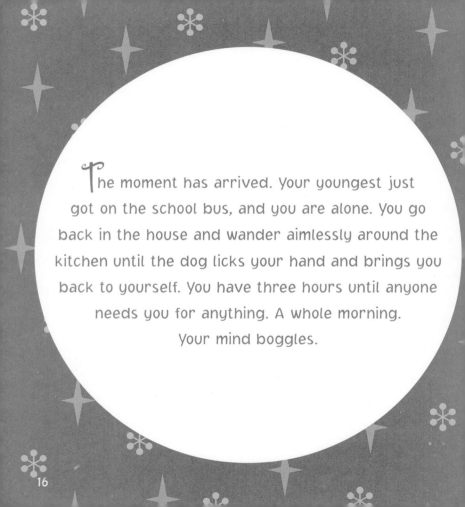

The moment has arrived. Your youngest just got on the school bus, and you are alone. You go back in the house and wander aimlessly around the kitchen until the dog licks your hand and brings you back to yourself. You have three hours until anyone needs you for anything. A whole morning. Your mind boggles.

"The way I look at it, if the kids are still alive when my husband comes home from work, then I've done my job."

—Roseanne

"Motherhood is like Albania—
you can't trust the
descriptions in the
books, you have
to go there."

—Marni Jackson

With firm resolve, you go into the room you like to think of as your studio, which strongly resembles a child's playroom, as do most rooms in the house, actually. It's a close shave—automatically, you begin to pick up, straighten up, and otherwise clean up—but no. This time is precious. You shove all the child-related items out of the line of sight from your worktable, and you prepare to create.

You close your eyes, kick off your shoes and the cat curls up at your feet. Suddenly, you're transported back to your first apartment, it's just you and your cat, and the world is yours. Yes! Your brain is still there! You set to work. You already can't wait to tell the kids about your day, while they tell you about theirs.

"'Mother' has always been a generic term synonymous with love, devotion, and sacrifice....They're the Walter Cronkites of the human race...infallible, virtuous, without flaws and conceived without original sin, with no room for ambivalence."

–Erma Bombeck

"Most mothers entering the labor market outside the home are naive. They stagger home each evening, holding mail in their teeth, the cleaning over their arm, a lamb chop defrosting under each armpit, balancing two gallons of frozen milk between their knees, and expect one of the kids to get the door."

—Erma Bombeck

"Can you come to school for a parent-teacher conference?" they requested. What do they mean, "conference?" Are they serious? A conference is where you set policies and plan strategies—but your daughter is only five, does she really require all that? You've started her college fund...what can they want to talk about? Is your daughter falling short in some way? It's hard to tell in schools, these days—what passes for a report card reads like stereo instructions. Is it about her behavior?

The school board used to be a little nervous about your escapades, until you single-handedly raised so much money to re-decorate the teacher's lounge that you ended up renovating it into a cappuccino bar and spa. Now you're the one they turn to for placing effective phone calls to the right people. They were undeniably impressed when the governor turned up for the annual fund-raiser, asking for the woman who really understood rock 'n roll.

"Adorable children
are considered to be
the general property
of the human race.
(Rude children belong
to their mothers.)"

—Judith Martin
  (Miss Manners)

"It's not easy being a mother. If it were easy, fathers would do it."

—Dorothy,
"The Golden Girls"

Okay, enough is enough. You know you're too busy when you realize that you haven't seen the bottoms of your feet for at least a month. You decide to go for it. Let them pound on the bathroom door; they're old enough to keep out of serious trouble (aren't they?). You run scalding hot bath water, while purposefully removing your shoes. Then one sock.
Then the other sock.

$\mathcal{D}$id you remember how cute your feet were? Your husband used to rave about them. With every fiber of your rebellious soul, you ignore the crash from the living room as you tenderly wash each toe in its turn. Toes are good; don't neglect them.

"Cleaning your house

while your kids

are still growing

is like shoveling

the walk before it

stops snowing."

–Phyllis Diller

"When her biographer says of an Italian woman poet, 'during some years her Muse was intermitted,' we do not wonder at the fact when he casually mentions her ten children."

—Anna Garlin Spencer

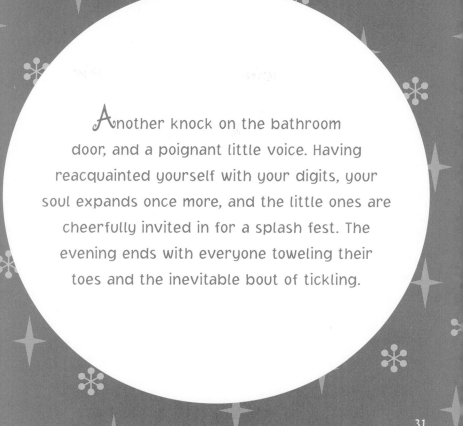

Another knock on the bathroom door, and a poignant little voice. Having reacquainted yourself with your digits, your soul expands once more, and the little ones are cheerfully invited in for a splash fest. The evening ends with everyone toweling their toes and the inevitable bout of tickling.

$\mathcal{M}$aybe it's time for a girls' night of poker. Encourage your friends to sit around in their undershirts and let their bellies hang out. When was the last time you had a pajama party with your girlfriends? Make sure there are plenty of pillows and chocolate chip cookies, and have everyone show up with a sleeping bag, flannel nightie or P.J.s, and their toothbrush. Maybe they'll need to go home at 11:00 p.m. to make sure the house hasn't burned down, but you'll have a blast in the meantime.

"When I had my daughter, I learned what the sound of one hand clapping is—it's a woman holding an infant in one arm and a pen in the other."

—Kate Braverman

"My children...have been a constant joy to me (except on the days when they weren't)."

–Evelyn Fairbanks

*M*emories of the Virgin Islands come flooding back to you. What a great trip, just you and your husband, and the goats that insisted on sharing your campsite. You remember the beautiful water, the underwater clouds of silvery fish, the colors of the reef—and the taxi driver who just about killed you on your way from the airport. All kinds of local color.

Your husband never thought he would capture your heart—you were so rebellious and free spirited. But it was a whirlwind romance, and everything you did together was full of passion and joy. Your mind wanders over all those corners of the world the two of you made your own—the pier at midnight, the alley behind your favorite Italian restaurant, the top of the fire tower overlooking the mountain, that dark corridor in the Ripley's Believe-It-Or-Not museum...

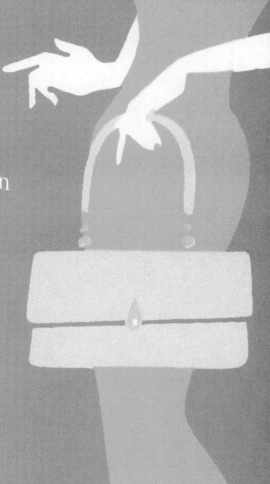

"You see
much more
of your children
once they
leave home."

–Lucille Ball

"There are times when parenthood seems nothing more than feeding the hand that bites you."

—Peter De Vries

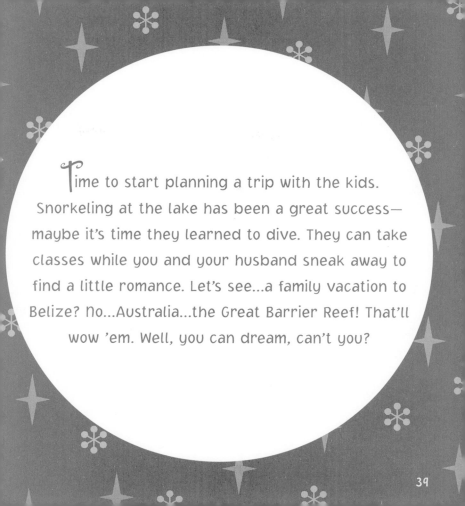

Time to start planning a trip with the kids. Snorkeling at the lake has been a great success—maybe it's time they learned to dive. They can take classes while you and your husband sneak away to find a little romance. Let's see...a family vacation to Belize? No...Australia...the Great Barrier Reef! That'll wow 'em. Well, you can dream, can't you?

39

Okay, this isn't looking good. You had to brag, didn't you? No roller coaster too tough for you, hey? How far up does this thing go? Has anyone died on this ride? Is it safe to do this to your ovaries? Why didn't you ask these questions before you accepted your son's dare? He's chatting calmly, the rat. Then, you plummet; you invert; you scream as though you've lost your mind.... Back on the ground, heart pounding, you smooth your hair and walk away on wobbly legs. But your son is beaming—it was worth it.

"If you can keep your head while all about you are losing theirs, it's just possible you haven't grasped the situation."

—Jean Kerr

"One mother...was taken aback when she called, as her daughter was going out the door, 'Have a good time,' and her daughter angrily replied, 'Stop telling me what to do!'"

—Nancy Samalin

You're the kind of person who can make waiting at the dentist's office fun. You started off making up stories with the kids and ended by making friends with everybody in the waiting room. They all wanted to be part of your continuous story game—there was even the lady who came back to join in again after her appointment was over.

Because you're a wild woman, seriously consider a toe-ring. Show it off as much as possible. Have a toenail painting party with your daughter, or with a group of friends. Include the dog. It's great bonding, and every time you look at your feet, you'll remember you're a cool mom.

"Mothers...

are basically

a patient lot.

They have to be

or they would

devour their offspring

early on, like guppies."

—Mary Daheim

"The trick, which requires the combined skills of a tightrope walker and a cordon bleu chef frying a plain egg, is to take your preteen daughter seriously without taking everything she says and does every minute seriously."

—Stella Chess

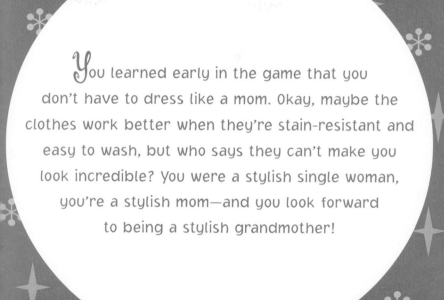

You learned early in the game that you don't have to dress like a mom. Okay, maybe the clothes work better when they're stain-resistant and easy to wash, but who says they can't make you look incredible? You were a stylish single woman, you're a stylish mom—and you look forward to being a stylish grandmother!

47

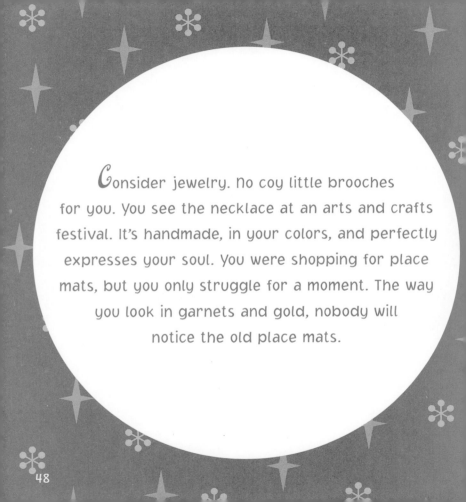

*C*onsider jewelry. No coy little brooches for you. You see the necklace at an arts and crafts festival. It's handmade, in your colors, and perfectly expresses your soul. You were shopping for place mats, but you only struggle for a moment. The way you look in garnets and gold, nobody will notice the old place mats.

"Why not have your first baby at sixty, when your husband is already dead and your career is over? Then you can really devote yourself to it."

—Fran Lebowitz

"Motherhood...

is the only journey

I've ever experienced

during which, in the

evening, I can already

feel nostalgic about

something that happened

that afternoon."

-Roberta Proctor

Then there's Victoria's Secret.
Perhaps her secret is she knows women
with children are illogically drawn to buy sexy
negligees, even though it may be years before
they have a chance to wear them. Try on as much as
you like, even if you don't buy anything. Better yet,
buy everything that looks good on you. It will not
go to waste on a wild woman like you.

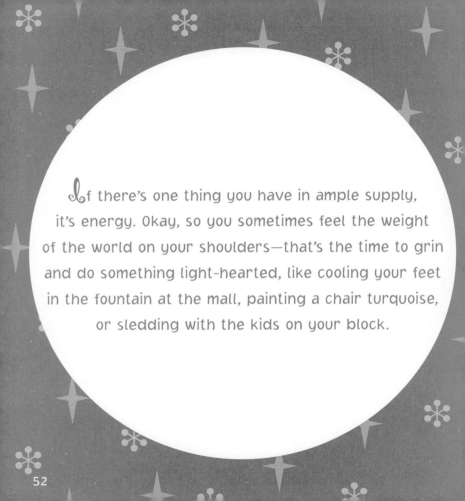

If there's one thing you have in ample supply, it's energy. Okay, so you sometimes feel the weight of the world on your shoulders—that's the time to grin and do something light-hearted, like cooling your feet in the fountain at the mall, painting a chair turquoise, or sledding with the kids on your block.

"If only we could

have them back

as babies today,

now that we have

some idea what

to do with them."

—Nancy Mairs

"I had never been as resigned to ready-made ideas as I was to ready-made clothes, perhaps because although I couldn't sew, I could think."

—Jane Rule

When you notice your friends are really getting down in the dumps, it's time for a truly trashy evening of indulgence to cheer yourselves up. Read trashy novels aloud, laugh at tacky magazines, eat frozen dinners. Rent a naughty movie, or at least one that's so bad it's funny. Indulge in the silliest, most fun entertainment you can think of. Read tabloids. Scratch lottery tickets. Play bingo. Eat chocolate and french fries and laugh at yourselves.

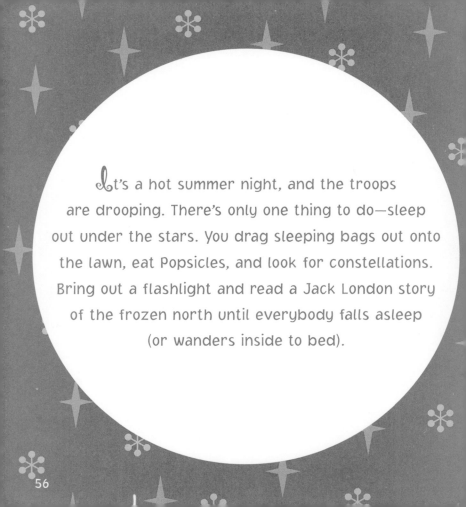

It's a hot summer night, and the troops are drooping. There's only one thing to do—sleep out under the stars. You drag sleeping bags out onto the lawn, eat Popsicles, and look for constellations. Bring out a flashlight and read a Jack London story of the frozen north until everybody falls asleep (or wanders inside to bed).

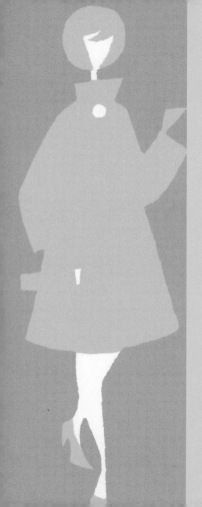

"How is a kid going to develop lung power if every little whimper makes Mom come running? My recommendation: keep the baby monitor you got as a gift and put it under the guest bed—lots more fun!"

–Cathy Crimmins

"A waist is a
terrible thing to mind."

–Jane Caminos

There are times when nothing will do
but to go out dancing. The kids are thrilled to
have a night at home with their favorite baby-sitter
(go on, admit it), and think it's hilarious that you and
dad still want to have dates. They are awestruck
when they see what you're wearing, and your
daughter considers not letting you leave the house.
You connect with your partner, you laugh with
friends—you know what? This could become
a regular occurrence!

How many moms keep a pair of roller-blades and a kite in the car—for themselves? You're a happy-go-lucky kind of girl, and you know the value of a spontaneous picnic. So you grab a backpack and head for the hills. It may be peanut butter and jelly sandwiches on a rock by a stream, or ham and cheese while you people-watch in the park, but you make life sparkle, you make life fun, and you will never be an ordinary mom.